BREAKTHROUGH

Power-packed Quotes From One of the World's Most Dynamic Preachers

by
Rod Parsley

Albury Publishing
Tulsa, Oklahoma

BREAKTHROUGH
Power-packed Quotes From One of the World's Most Dynamic Preachers

ISBN 1-57778-015-9

Published by Albury Publishing
P. O. Box 470406
Tulsa, Oklahoma 74147

All of the quotes in this publication were taken from
Rod Parsley's teachings or from the following books:

Holiness: Living Leaven Free
The Commanded Blessing
Tribulation to Triumph
God's Answer to Insufficient Funds
Ten Golden Keys to Your Abundance
Repairers of the Breach
My Promise Is the Palace, So What Am I Doing in the Pit?
The Backside of Calvary
Free at Last
Serious Survival Strategies for Victory
Praise and Worship

BREAKTHROUGH

YOUR breakthrough will occur
when you receive the advanced
knowledge of God that will
propel you through *every* line
of Satan's defenses.

4

I'M not an abnormal person living in a normal world... I'm a normal person living in an abnormal world.

WHAT if this is the one day
your need met His miracle?

RIGHT now you can make
a decision! You can allow your
mountain to move your faith
or you can allow your faith
to move your mountain.

WHY don't you get alone until...you're not alone anymore.

8

WHAT'S happening
in you is greater than what's
happening *to* you.

9

IT is not what we wear on the outside that matters, but what burns in the sanctuary of our hearts.

QUIT trying to see how close
you can live to the world and
still be saved. It is time to get
the sin out of our lives.

THE atmosphere of expectancy is the breeding ground of miracles.

BREAKTHROUGH

A *breakthrough* is a sudden burst of the advanced knowledge of God which is able to propel you through every line of Satan's defenses.

WHENEVER evil mires the work of God, our flesh reasserts itself and our lack of fruit condemns our prayerless, power-less, passionless Christianity. We need another drenching, downpour of Pentecostal power.

14

GOD wants us to be accountable — to be a people of our word — to give a day's work for a day's pay.

SIN has gratification...
for a moment.
But hell lasts...
for eternity!

16

WE can be cleansed of the mud of this world through the washing of the Word and the blood of Jesus. Let Jesus cleanse the mud from your life.

INSTEAD of asking, "What fellowship does light have with darkness?" it is time we start asking, "What fellowship could the devil possibly want with us?"

AS tongue-talking, on-fire,
Bible-believing, Holy Ghost-filled
children of Almighty God,
we shouldn't look, smell, or
taste good to the devil.

IF we cannot hear the voice
of God through a man of God —
and respond to that voice as
if God spoke directly to us —
then we are never going to
be able to clearly hear the
voice of God for ourselves.

BREAKTHROUGH

IN order to have an impact on our society, God is moving the body of Christ to rise far above the status quo of church as normal. We live in a society where the right has been wrong for so long that righteousness is the abnormal thing.

PARENTS, teach your children respect for authority. In the midst of the constant violence and negatives in television and the movies, let them see their authority figures doing the things of God in their lives.

EVERY fresh new golden era in human history has been preceded by the devotion and righteous passion of one or more individuals who knew their God and knew where they were going.

WE have not been building on the foundations of faith, hope, and love with Christ as the cornerstone. Instead, we have been building on fear and panic, putting our hope in political masterminds who have manipulated the unthinking, undiscerning masses to the perpetuation of their own perversion.

THIS generation needs discerning fathers who realize that the heart of the human problem is the problem of the human heart, and that the commission of our mission is to get the life of God into the hearts of humanity.

OUR worth to God in public depends upon what we are in private.

THE calling of God is a holy thing. Don't ever take the gifts and abilities given to us by God for granted.

IF we look to man to promote us, God never will. If we look to God to promote us, man has no choice.

MANY times, we are waiting for God to do something for us, but the promises of God are already accomplished facts.

IF God writes His word on our hearts, and our bodies are the temple of the Holy Ghost, it means the same presence of God that was inside the Holy of Holies is now inside us!

THERE are no angels going into the world preaching. The Holy Spirit Himself does not preach. Jesus told *us* to go into all the earth and preach the Gospel.

IF we are not getting answers, it isn't because God has stopped answering prayer but because we have forgotten to ask.

WE are invading enemy-held territory with all the arsenal of God at our disposal. Yet while some are brandishing swords and spears, others are waving butter knives.

33

THE baptism of the Holy Ghost will do for you what a phone booth did for Clark Kent — it will change you into a different human being.

HAVE you noticed that the world is plagued by more evil than ever before? The devil has turned up the heat and is intensifying his attack. Why? He knows the hour we are living in. The devil is running out of time.

SIN is the one thing we all have in common but nobody wants to talk about.

THE New Age movement is not new at all — it is one of the oldest lies on the face of the earth. It is Eastern mysticism dressed up in Western clothing.

37

THE first step to freedom
is confession.

38

YOU cannot turn *from* something unless you turn *toward* something. When we repent, we are leaving something behind and going on to something else.

REPENTANCE is not penance. You do not have to do anything to make God forgive you. You do not have to cry. You do not have to kneel until your feet are numb. All you have to do is obey the Word of God.

WE are the generation destined for the experimental manifestation and revelation of the glory of God.

JESUS will lead you into the land, but it becomes your responsibility to possess it.

THE devil is not nervous about churches with a weather-worn sign hanging on some shanty where twelve people for the last fifteen years have come together to talk about nothing.

43

BREAKTHROUGH

A night vision is different from a dream. A dream is because you ate too much pizza. A night vision is because God is trying to impart something to your spirit.

44

BREAKTHROUGH

I'M not ashamed to tell you that there is only one way to God, and that is through the blood of His Son. I'm not ashamed to tell you that hell is hot and eternity is long.

PEOPLE have said that it's selfish to ask God to give a hundredfold return on the seeds sown in the financial realm. No, it's selfish *not* to expect the hundredfold return. Having just enough for your own needs will never bless anyone else.

46

BREAKTHROUGH

IF you need something today that you didn't have yesterday, then you have to learn to do something different today from the way you were doing it yesterday.

GREAT men of God don't fall — we let go of them.

WE do not receive grace by signing someone's church roll. We do not receive it by going to church and sitting on the front row. You do not have any more of it than I do, and I do not have any more of it than you do. It is the free gift of God.

49

THE Holy God, the Creator of the universe, gives us free access into His presence! The veil that hung in the temple, four-inches thick, woven without seam, twenty-feet wide, and forty-feet high, was torn from top to bottom by God, and He said, "I am coming out, and you are coming in."

HUMILITY is the greatest character-building stone known in the arsenal of God, and grace humbles us. Character is the product of grace.

GOD is far bigger than our
ability to please Him.

52

CHARACTER is built within us because we know Who God is and, therefore, we know who we are.

GOD shed His precious blood on Calvary for us, and the price has been paid. Period.

IMMORTALITY is what separates Christianity from every other form of religion in the world – because we are going to live forever in the pavilions of God, walking on streets of gold, hearing the angelic song, and marching and dancing to the song of the redeemed throughout the endless ages of eternity.

55

WE are bought with a price,
and man did not pay it!
God shed His precious blood
on Calvary for us, and He is
the only One we need to please!

SALVATION is by grace. Salvation comes by the blood of the cross of Christ. Nothing less and nothing more.

FOR too long we have been believing God for a little trickle of blessing while the flood tide of the glory of God is pouring over the sapphire sill of heaven's gate, and splashing the sides of the earth. Do not miss it.

GOD wants to give you
a significant breakthrough...
that thing you have desired for so
long, you have almost forgotten
how bad you wanted it.

THERE'S much to be gained from a return to the discarded values of the past. Thank God for men that are not just puppets, but men that will get behind the sacred pulpit of God and begin to cry out like prophets.

IF we received an unexpected thousand dollar bill, we would believe in emotionalism. So why not get emotional about Jesus? He owns the cattle on a thousand hills.

HONESTLY, it would not really matter to me if the gates of heaven were made of wood or if they swung on leather hinges. It would not matter to me if there was mud in the streets knee-deep, and the mansions were nothing more than cardboard shanties. Because, when I look down the end of that muddy street, at the end of that heavenly boulevard, I will see the One Who took my place.

IN a time when a powerless Pentecost has been the norm and not the exception, with more perversion than power, more playboys than prophets and more compromise than conviction, we need the Holy Ghost who condescends to indwell mortals and fill us full of Himself.

So many people are confused about the last book of the Bible, but there is no reason to be confused about it. In fact, if there is any generation in the history of the world that should understand the book of Revelation — it is this one.

WE are watching prophecy being fulfilled every day. We don't need the evening news. Just read the Bible, and you will know the news before it happens.

TO God, your dark tomb of tribulation is just the fertile ground from which He will resurrect your deliverance.

OUR job is to learn not only *of* God, but also *from* God, that we might tell others *about* God, so all men can be drawn closer *to* God.

THERE are still those who ask, "Is God even *able* to heal?" *Able?!* He set the world spinning upside down and commanded the oceans not to spill a drop. When your body isn't functioning correctly, who better is there to turn to than the One Who created you?

MANY who claim they have experienced the baptism of the Holy Ghost are more dead than alive, more off than on, more wrong than right. Some are more spirit frilled than spirit filled. We have been used to the "outer fringe of His works" and have forgotten the "inner essence of His power."

GET a Word from God – *and stick with it.* Even if you have to paper your walls with little yellow "stick'em" notes, keep His Words of faith and healing always before you.

SIN is sly. It works much like a cat playing with a ball of yarn. It's fun for a little while. But before you know it, its cords of death will have wrapped around you, and you will find yourself entangled by your despair.

MARRIAGE is a union between two imperfect individuals who, despite their imperfections, make a covenant with one another to stick it out.

PERHAPS the first voice to ever utter "power to the people" was the Holy Spirit as He rode into the city on the very breath of God.

IF God can use a donkey, He can use you!

WHAT we call dysfunctional homes the Bible calls a generational curse.

THE anointing is like a spiritual deodorant. It is our safeguard against the attack of rotten, stinking sin.

THE world doesn't need another gifted man. It is looking for a yielded man, an anointed man.

WE are not to serve God
just because He made us.
We are to serve Him because
He gave us the right to choose
whom we would serve.

WHEN you pour out your hopes and dreams at the feet of Jesus, the rewards can only be measured by the light of eternity.

THE Church has become professional in doing the work of the Lord, but it has forgotten the Lord of the work! What God wants from us is not religion, but relationship.

THE best minds cannot compete with a blessed mind!

WE worship a God Who enjoys unique, colorful, and beautiful things. He longs to beautify us. He desires that we stand out in a crowd and display His glory. When God blesses us, He is showing us off.

WE say we are weak —
God says you're wicked. We say
we are sick — God says you sin.

IT doesn't matter if the doctor looks at you and says you have to die and cannot live. Begin to seek God for the anointing. Your darkest hour will soon be like the glistening radiance of the noonday sun.

WHEN God spoke, darkness responded. It had to dissipate at the sound of His voice.

I don't believe the Church has lost its appetite, but the appetites have changed. People have forgotten how to wait in the presence of the Lord while He prepares and serves up exactly what their souls are longing for.

WHEN a mother loudly says *No!* or slaps her baby's hand as it reaches for a hot oven, she is protecting her child. When God gave His commandments to His children, He was doing the same thing. The commandments of God were given for our protection.

MOST people want revival so they can see miracles. Many come to special services hoping for signs and wonders. How many come because the Lover of their soul is going to show up and they just want to catch a glimpse of Him?

YOU are not to go after
other gods and serve them.
You probably have not erected
a shrine in your back yard.
But what about that one sitting in
your family room with antennae
horns and an electric cord tail?

WHEN you are obedient,
you will be so prosperous that you
will have money to lend to others
who are less fortunate than you.
You won't need *MasterCard*
– you just need the Master!

ONCE you have recognized that His Word was given just for you, the impact of such love will overwhelm you. You will forget *what* you are, because you will be caught up in *Whose* you are.

YOU do not know what the devil has plotted against you tomorrow, so pray in the Holy Ghost today.

THE world has been lying well, and we have been telling the truth badly.

WE draw our strength from the battle. From our greatest conflicts come our greatest victories!

IF you're going to survive the perils of perilous times, you need to have a faith that knows. You need to have a faith that grows. You need to have a faith that's rooted.

Do not blame your
inconsistencies on God;
He has never failed.

TO feed your spirit man, study the Word of God. Memorize it. Let it sink deep into your spirit. It is the most tangible and powerful weapon God has given us for our spiritual arsenal.

I believe those chariots that have not ridden the wind since the days of Elijah are being polished by the heavenly hosts and preparing to be pulled out of their stalls.
I believe Jesus is coming — soon.

BREAKTHROUGH

IN the midst of the trials of life,
it is one thing to know God. It is
another thing to have God say,
"I know this man, I know his heart,
and I know he will faithfully serve
me." I want to be that man.

SATAN is not original.
What he has done to others,
he will try to do to you.

WHEN you know the strategies of Satan, he cannot take you by surprise. When you know there is a spiritual war going on, you will not be vulnerable to the attack of the enemy.

$\mathbf{A}$ wise saint once said,
"The only way you can tell if
Satan is lying is if his lips move."

OUR chromium plated,
over organized, stream lined,
computerized form of Christianity
has been as effective as trying to
melt an iceberg with a match stick.

103

HOW much time have you spent in prayer lifting up the arms of others? We must stop demanding so much more of everyone else than we do of ourselves.

WE have sacrificed the standard of righteousness and holiness for loose living and corrupt consciences. We have so deluged ourselves in political policies we have forgotten Biblical basics. We have sacrificed what is right on the altar of what is politically correct.

105

INSTEAD of carrying spiritual machine guns, many Christians are going into battle with squirt guns. This is spiritual life and death. It is not playing around; it is not take it or leave it. Your life depends on this.

WHILE the homosexuals are "coming out of the closet" Christians are "running to the closet" because they don't want to "clean out their closet."

WHEN the trials of your faith come, and you feel like bowing down under their weight, remember the three Hebrew children and the fiery furnace. They did not bow, and they did not burn.

PRAYER is our communication link with the Lord. The plan of God is this: He wants you to stay within calling distance.

WITHOUT prayer, you are like a blindfolded soldier without a weapon – unable to see the enemy, and without the firepower to destroy him.

110

WE have so lowered the standards of spiritual anointing that what we are now aiming for was once under our feet.

DO you know what FEAR is?
False Evidence that Appears Real.
It is an illusion. Be full of faith,
not full of fear.

GOD said that in the last days it is going to get horrific — it will take a bag of gold to buy a piece of bread. Let the economies collapse; if it takes a bag of gold to buy a slice of bread, we will own the bakery.

GREATER is my God Who is in me, in front of me, behind me, beside me, beneath me, above me, than the devil that is in the world.

WHEN we go where we should
not go, we are going to see what we
should not see. When we go where
we should not go, we are going to
do what we should not do.
Most of the time, we cause
our own problems.

115

STAY faithful to God — never quit — never allow bitterness or anger to set in your spirit — and your life will become a living temple to glorify His Holy name.

MY deep definition
of sovereignty –
He is God, and you are not!

THE true representation of your character is not how you respond on the mountaintop; but how you respond to the raging fires and floods of life.

GREAT revelation doesn't come without great preparation.

119

JUST as a river flows on a steady course, God, your Father, has a well-designed plan for you.

WE serve a God who supplies *before* there is a need. You don't have to wait for a blessing. He has *already* anointed your head with oil.

BEFORE you can receive what is in God's hand, you first have to unclench your fist and offer the Lord what is in your hand.

RIGHTEOUSNESS
is what God does. Holiness is what we do. He deals with our character; we deal with our conduct.

GOD'S kingdom is a theocracy, not a democracy. It's not up for a vote. Christ is our King, and we are His loyal subjects.

TWO of the greatest barriers to blessing are stubbornness and conceit. Those who believe they have all the answers don't leave much room for God.

WHAT would you attempt for God if you knew it was impossible to fail? Well, what's stopping you?

FASTING is not a hunger strike against God — trying to persuade Him to do something, or wanting Him to feel sorry for you because you haven't eaten. Instead, it is a denial of self that brings you to a point where you can align your spirit with what God already intends to do.

127

GOD is not worried about how much land you own; He wants to know about your productivity. Results are more important than acreage.

TALKING about your past should not be used as an opportunity to show off your scars, but as a time to speak with humility about your experiences.

EVERYTHING we have is the result of the mercy of God.

I didn't start with million-dollar faith. I couldn't count that high. God took me from where I was to where He wanted me to be.

BELIEVING with your heart and speaking with your mouth are the two hinges on which the door of abundance swings.

IF you want to experience God's abundance, find a church where their sword is not just being polished, but is dripping with the blood of the enemy – where it has pierced the heart and soul of the demonic forces of hell. Get involved with those who are in the heat of the battle.

133

THE *same Jesus* who healed the woman with an issue of blood, who cleansed ten lepers in Samaria, who opened the eyes of blind Bartimaeus, *has the same power today.* He is still in the healing business.

IT'S God's money before you ever give it. Somehow we need to break the mindset that we are giving to men. No. We are returning to God what is already His.

GOD doesn't tell us to "Figure it out," He says, "Go!" He didn't tell Joshua, "Get out your calculators and physics books to see what combination of pitch and vibration we need to make these walls of Jericho fall down." He said, "March! and blow those horns!"

PRESENTING your offering to the priest who is currently in office should be as natural as saying "Amen" in church. It's an ordinance established by the Lord.

FAR too often, we keep for ourselves the best and offer to the Lord that which costs us little. Five percent is not ten percent. Give your best to God and prepare to see His abundance released into your life.

WHEN Christians across the land move into obedience, our entire nation will be transformed. God will look down from His holy habitation and grant blessing after blessing.

THE ark of the covenant was more than wood, cloth, and precious stones. It was anointed by God. Those things that are sanctified and dedicated to the Lord take on a significance far greater than the physical elements they possess.

WHEN you tithe, you are not just placing paper in a plate. You are returning something to God as an act of faith and worship. Let me tell you a secret. When God touches that little piece of paper He can multiply it until a mountain of obligations disappear.

141

DO you know why the Dead Sea has its name? It takes water in, but it doesn't give any out. It's dead. It's not wise to be only a taker and not a giver.

SIN was introduced into the world when one man reached for an apple under a tree. The cure for sin was birthed by another Man who hung on a tree for you and me.

YOUR real battle takes place in the spirit world — where God has given you the power to pull down every earthly stronghold!

THE only sin God cannot forgive is unconfessed sin.

I am tired of the Church looking like the world, talking like the world, acting like the world. It is time we become established in the holiness of God and live where the evil one cannot touch us.

THE process of life is the process of exchange. God cannot pour more into us until we let some out.

REMEMBER, God defines death as separation from Him; hence, life would mean to be in His presence.

THERE is only one way to receive salvation, and that is to recognize you are a sinner in need of the blood of a Savior.

FAITH sees what cannot be seen, hears what cannot be heard. Faith changes you into a human being who can believe what cannot be believed, who can see what cannot be seen, and who can hear what cannot be heard.

RECONCILIATION is to exchange from hatred to friendship – an act of God which enables man to fellowship with Him.

151

WE serve a sovereign God, and He is in control. He did not pay half price for you. God paid FULL PRICE, and He has a plan and a purpose for your life!

GOD knows who you are, and He has a predestined, divine assignment for your life. His desire is to take you out of the pit and put you into the palace!

ONCE you grasp God's vision for your life you will no longer be satisfied with church as usual. You won't be satisfied with a six-foot icicle standing behind the pulpit spouting his three points and a poem. You will cry, "Where are the signs and wonders? Where are the miracles? Where is the revelation and the demonstration?"

WHEREVER you are –
pit, path, or palace – you have been
preordained to climb to the glory
and blessing of Almighty God!

HE is God, and you are not. There are many today who try to convince you that you are God....but when was the last time you walked across the water in your swimming pool, displaying your omnipotence?

IF you put all of God's
characteristics into a pot and boiled
them down, they would boil down
to one all-encompassing element
of His divine nature: LOVE.

ABOUT THE AUTHOR

Rod Parsley began his ministry as an energetic 19-year-old, in the backyard of his parents' Ohio home. The fresh, "old-time Gospel" approach of Parsley's delivery immediately attracted a hungry, God-seeking audience. From the 17 people who attended that first backyard meeting, the crowds grew rapidly.

Today, as the pastor of Columbus, Ohio's 5,200-seat World Harvest Church, Parlsey oversees World Harvest's Preschool-12 Christian Academy; World Harvest Bible College; numerous church-sponsored outreaches; and Breakthrough, World Harvest Church's daily and weekly television broadcast, currently available to 96% of the populations of the United States and parts of Canada.

For information on other books
offered by Albury Publishing, write:

Albury Publishing
P. O. Box 470406
Tulsa, Oklahoma 74147-0406

To contact the author write:
Rod Parsley
World Harvest Church
P. O. Box 32932
Columbus, Ohio 43232-0932
USA